LORD ABERNATHY FINDS A HOME

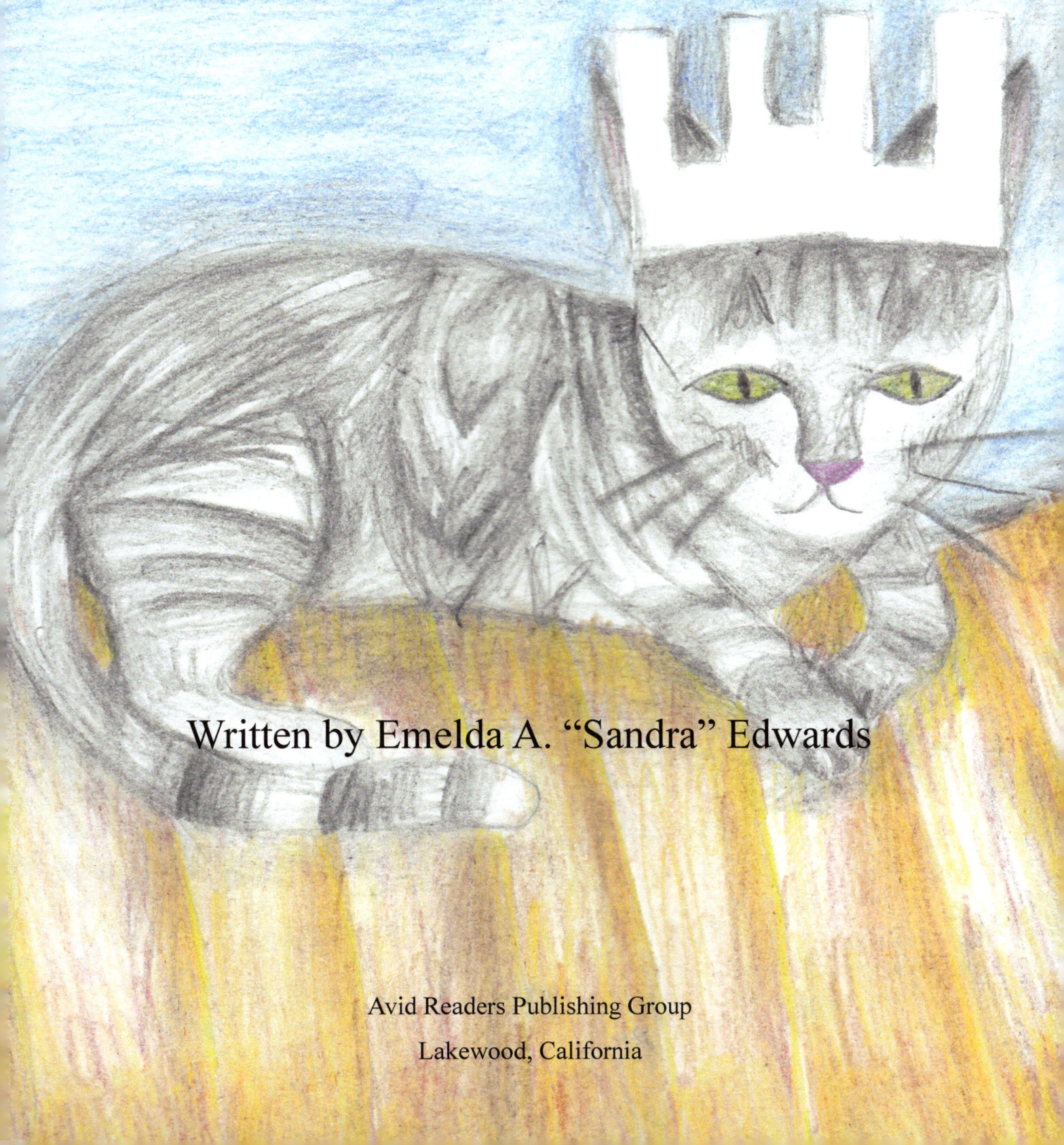

Written by Emelda A. "Sandra" Edwards

Avid Readers Publishing Group

Lakewood, California

Lord Abernathy Finds A Home

EDITED by Bernice R. Smith Hall

Illustrations by: Keyvil Alexis King, St. Joseph's High School

Jaina Warren, St. Joseph's High School

Chelsea Beaupierre, St. Joseph's High School

Avid Readers Publishing Group

http://www.avidreaderspg.com

ISBN-13: 978-1-61286-259-0

Printed in the United States

Lord Abernathy Finds A Home

"Lord Abernathy, Lord Abernathy! Where are you hiding now?"

Oh, oh. That's me.

Hello. My name is Lord Abernathy. I'm a dark grey and light grey, handsome kitten and I'm nine weeks old. I was living at the animal shelter on the beautiful island of St. Croix in the Virgin Islands when, one Sunday morning, a nice lady came to the shelter and saw me. I was five weeks old and she could not resist me, so she decided to take me home with her. I can tell you, it's like heaven having all this space to explore and frolic in. It's no fun being cooped up in a tiny cage.

It was a bit difficult the first day or two in my new home. Come on. I was just a baby, so there were…ahem…accidents on the bathroom mats, the bottom of the curtains and other areas. Well, the nice lady set me straight after a few mishaps. She showed me how to use the litter box when I needed to relieve myself by scratching my front paws in the kitty litter and it has been smooth sailing…I mean, smooth scratching from then on.

At meal time, I had to be fed with a dropper since I was not yet able to drink milk or water from a bowl. On the first day at my new home, the nice lady fed me sardines in tomato sauce. Even though I could not drink milk or water from a bowl, I certainly was able to lap up the tomato sauce and even eat some of the sardines. Well, I had a slight case of diarrhea after that meal. Now look at me. I can eat and drink from my bowl.

Life is one big playground for me. My only wish is for a brother or sister to play with. Since I don't have a playmate, I am contented chewing on the nice lady's hands.

There are two other cats in residence but they are very hostile toward me. One is called Bobsey and the other is Little Girl. Bobsey is a big, black and white monster! I tried to play with him but he growled fiercely and slapped me. Imagine, that beast could be my granddaddy and he wants to fight a little bundle of joy like me. Look at him. He's eating my food! I don't know why he's always snarling and growling, so I am staying far away from that bad, old Bobsey.

Little Girl is no young chick. She's been around for many years and her coat is all dark grey. She was given her name because she's petite. I have tried to play with her, but she is unfriendly and prefers to stay in a corner by herself.

5

In my new home there is plenty of room, food and love for all three of us, but those two felines are strange at best. I don't think they're related by birth, but they are both grouches. I think Bobsey is the problem. He is just savage. I believe Little Girl remains in the corner to avoid getting in his way. She is not giving him a chance to slap her. Well, I can play by myself and the nice lady lets me chew on her hands.

"Get out of my flower garden, Lord Abernathy! Leave my plants alone! Out, Abernathy!"

Oh, oh. It's always don't do this, Abernathy or don't do that, Abernathy. Why can't I do all the fun things like swing on the curtains, or bite the electrical cord, or go to the bathroom on the potted house plants? The nice lady is a party pooper but I still love her.

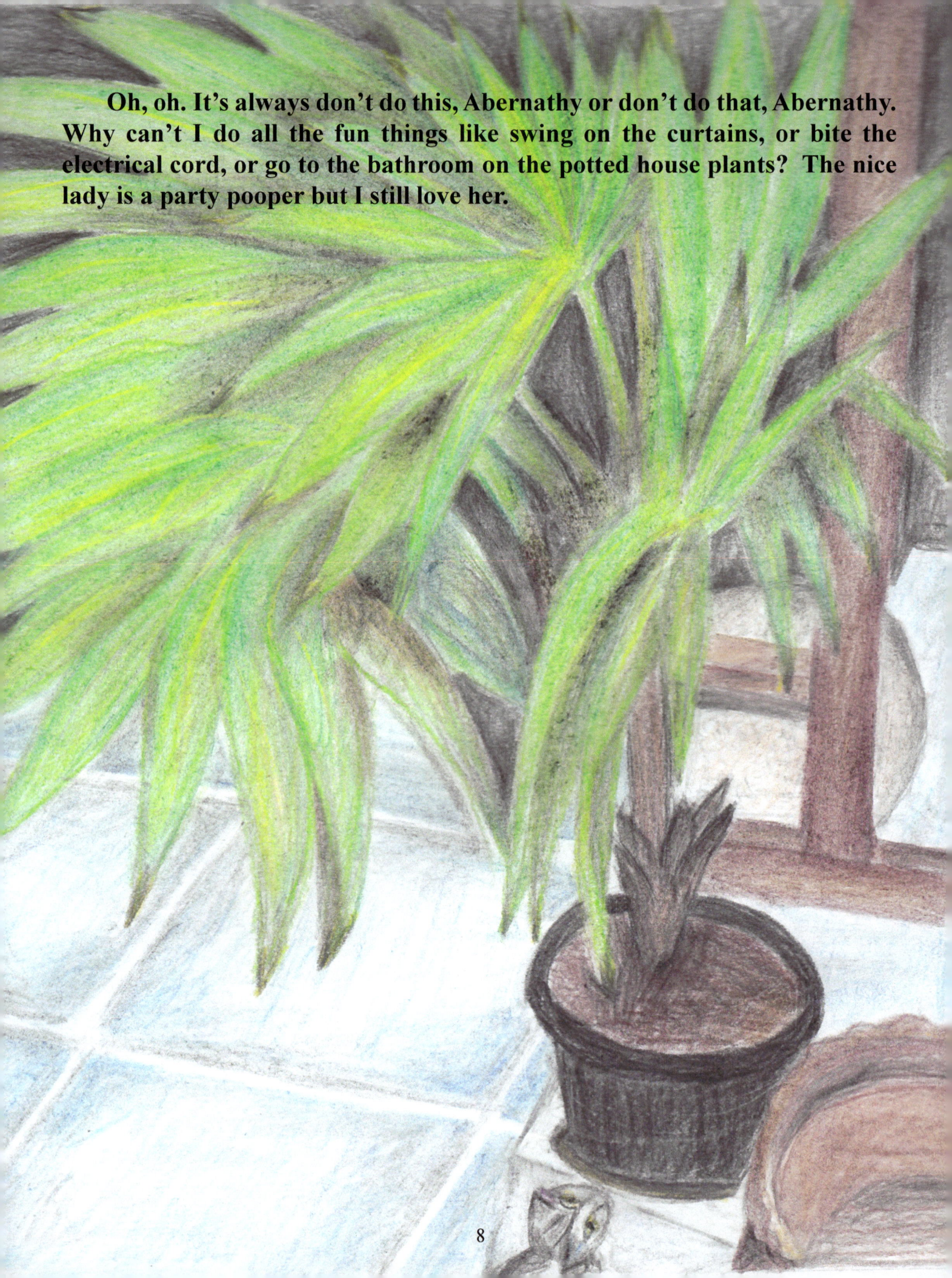

Oh, no! Not another bath. Oh, well. I guess I'll grin and bear it.

The nice lady accidentally stepped on my back paw and it was painful for a few days. I lost my appetite and was not eating much and the nice lady was worried. She soaked my paw in warm salt water and rubbed it with aloes and nursed me back to health. The pain went away and I am my old self again.

Hey, don't think that I'm laughing here, because I'm not! It is chow time and I'm letting the nice lady know that I'm hungry.

The nice lady lets me go outdoors every day. She makes sure that I stay on the carport. One day I followed Little Girl into the street. The nice lady rushed out, grabbed me and scolded me. I learned never to go into the street and to always stay close to home.

Because of the two grouches, the nice lady puts me in the bathroom with food, water and my litter box when she goes to work. She hates to lock me in, but she is afraid that Bobsey will hurt me while she is gone. I don't like being locked in, so one day I hid under the bed and would not come out when she called me. But she knew how to get me out. She knows that I like to go outside, so she made a lot of noise while opening the kitchen door. When I heard the door being opened, I rushed out and she caught me and put me in the bathroom. When she goes to run short errands, she takes me with her. I get nervous riding in the car, but it is better than being locked in the bathroom.

Oh, look! Another kitty to play with. She sure is cute, but why is she hiding behind the mirror? Why doesn't she come out to play with me? Oh, well. I guess she is just another meanie like the two grouches.

"Lord Abernathy, you are looking at yourself in the mirror."

Why do we have to be mean to each other? We must learn to love and accept each other regardless of our differences. Being kind to each other makes life better for everyone and makes the world a happier place in which to live. From now on I will stop referring to Bobsey and Little Girl as grouches.

Now, what is the nice lady doing? What is she putting on my head?

"Keep still, Lord Abernathy. Let me get this crown on your head."

I don't want anything on my head. I just want to get some much-needed sleep. Anyway, I'm an American, so why the British name?

Ah, blessed sleep. I'm so tired from telling my story.

When I wake up, it will be back to fun and frolic and I will find ways to be kind to Bobsey and Little Girl. I know the nice lady will laugh at my antics.

THE END

www.ingramcontent.com/pod-product-compliance
Lightning Source LLC
Chambersburg PA
CBHW041559040426

42447CB00002B/234